BONDSLAVE

*The Inconvenient Truth About
Your Identity in Christ*

By
Rolland Wright

© 2020 by Rolland Wright. All rights reserved. No part of this book may be transmitted or reproduced in any form, or by any means, mechanical or electronic, including photocopying, without written permission of Rolland Wright.

ALL RIGHTS RESERVED. This book contains material protected under International and Federal Laws and Treaties. Any unauthorized reprint or use of this material is prohibited. No portion of this book may be used, reproduced, stored in a retrieval system, or transmitted in any form or by any means — electronic, mechanical, photocopy, recording, scanning, or other — without express written permission from the authors or publisher, except for brief quotation in critical reviews or articles. It is illegal to copy this book, post it to a website, or distribute it by any other means without permission from the authors and publisher.

Published by

Wright Publishing Company
3616 Colby Ave. #788, Everett, WA 98201
Phone: 844-494-3697
Website: www.firstplaceministries.com
Email: Rolland@firstplaceministries.com

Copyright Use and Public Information

Unless otherwise noted, images have been used according to public information laws.

ISBN: 978-1-7362169-9-6 Paperback

Limits of Liability and Disclaimer of Warranty The author and publisher shall not be liable for the reader's misuse of this material. This book is for strictly informational and educational purposes.

Scripture quotations taken from the New American Standard Bible® (NASB), Copyright © 1960, 1962, 1963, 1968, 1971, 1972, 1973, 1975, 1977, 1995 by The Lockman Foundation Used by permission. www.Lockman.org. Scriptures marked NIV are taken from the NEW INTERNATIONAL VERSION (NIV): Scripture taken from THE HOLY BIBLE, NEW INTERNATIONAL VERSION ®. Copyright© 1973, 1978, 1984, 2011 by Biblica, Inc.™. Used by permission of Zondervan. Scriptures taken from the Tree of Life version © 2015 by the Messianic Jewish Family Bible Society. Used by permission of the Messianic Jewish Family Bible Society. "TLV" and "Tree of Life Version" and "Tree of Life Holy Scriptures" are trademarks registered in the United States Patent and Trademark office by the Messianic Family Bible Society.

Disclaimer

The views expressed are those of the author and do not reflect the official policy or position of the publisher or The Widows Project This publication is designed to provide accurate and authoritative information regarding the subject matter covered. It is sold with the understanding that the publisher is not engaged in rendering legal, accounting, clinical or other professional advice. If legal advice or other expert assistance is required, the services of a competent professional should be sought. The opinions expressed by the authors in this book are not endorsed by The Widows Project, and are the sole responsibility of the author rendering the opinion.

ENDORSEMENTS

The apostle Paul embraced the concept of "dying to self". In fact, he proclaimed the self-necessity of "dying daily." In each of his letters, he and a host of other's self-identified as "bond-slaves" of Jesus Christ. They were compelled to live a radical life of faith in Jesus. Can we do any less? Are we not commanded by the Master Himself?

Rolland adeptly exhorts us to embrace our identity in Christ Jesus.

– Brother Steve Anderson

My hunger for the Lord compels me to want to be on time and in season with His purposes in the earth and if you do too you must read this book. Mr. Wright's revelation on where the Body of Christ (Ekklesia) is and where we are in history as humanity is very, very eye opening and encouraging. I highly recommend it.

– Sharon Best
Wife, Mom, Grandmother (Ammy)
Certified Life Coach
Certified Restoring The Foundations Minister
Facilitator of Ekklesia War Room

DEDICATION

I want to dedicate this book to my parents who have modeled an unparalleled consistency and perseverance of devotion in their lives with Jesus Christ. They have lived quiet lives and worked with their hands. I thank you for your example.

ACKNOWLEDGEMENTS

For me, this portion of the book is more difficult to write than the content. It creates a certain anxiety. I am fearful of not mentioning someone who is certainly worthy of acknowledging.

As I reflect on my life, the awareness of being a slave of Jesus has been a lifetime process that led up to a pivotal moment of self-discovery, repentance, reconciliation, restoration and repurposing.

So many people have had an influence in my life, but the single greatest catalyst was Sandra Hyatt. Her transparency in front of a congregation modeled James 5:16 (TLV) "So confess your offenses (sins) to one another and pray for one another so that you may be healed." Her testimony caused me to rush home that afternoon and draft an overview accounting of my life. It was not a pretty thing. The more I wrote, and the Holy Spirit revealed to me, the sicker I felt. I sent a copy of that document to Sandy and a good friend of mine, Bill Morris. The exercise in humility brought healing and correction. I am thankful for the forgiveness and mercy that Jesus extends to us when we repent. This book is the fruit of my confession.

I want to thank my friends in Lagos, Portugal who also impacted my life during the time this book was being formulated. Especially Maria Abrantes who introduced me to a host of friends including Michael and Yoka Findlay, Pastors of Oasis Christian Fellowship, Lois, Elizabeth, David, John, Ron and Ken. Also, Pastor Samuel and his family of Shalom Assembly.

I am grateful for my publisher and editors, Jim and Jackie Morey. You have impacted my life beyond your publishing skills. Thank you for your friendship and Ekklesia Fellowship.

TABLE OF CONTENTS

Foreword 1

Chapter 1 5
Are you a Slave? Or are you a Servant?

Chapter 2 17
Choose Today who you will Serve! Or Who is Your Master?

Chapter 3 21
Self-Identified as Slaves

Chapter 4 29
But what about…?

Chapter 5 35
Simple Stories, Profound Truths

Chapter 6 41
Conformed to His Image

Chapter 7 45
Open Your Eyes!

Chapter 8 55
A Seven Day Devotional

King James Version (Addendum) 67

15 Rules of Translation for the King James
Version (KJV) 73

About the Author 79

FOREWORD

It was during my Scripture studies in 2015 that the Holy Spirit drew my attention to an observation I made regarding a word contained in the first verse, of the first chapter, of most of the New Testament writers. While I did some research to satisfy my curiosity, I failed to investigate the word historically, allowing my angst to lay fallow for the time being. It would not be until the middle of 2020 while coming across a post on Facebook that I was struck by the title of a book, "***Leaving Church and Becoming Ekklesia.***"

I had spent most of the prior five years trying to make sense of my dissatisfaction with the organized church. I was unsettled and wrestling within my spirit. I wasn't looking to leave the organized church as I did for a while in the early 70's. The late 60's and 70's were a time of great change and turmoil in the United States. Not only was there political and philosophical strife but the Church was undergoing change too.

In 2015 I launched a nonprofit called ***The Widows Project***. Part of my frustration was fueled by difficulty in helping the Church to see the widow. I had discovered the Father's heart toward the widow, and the Church was walking past them, not noticing. Interesting enough, a dispute between the Greek widows and the Jewish widows arose (what I call the original Me2 movement) because "*their widows were being overlooked in the daily support.*" The tensions our nation is experiencing is not a new thing. But notice that we do not hear about this issue again in scripture. Apparently, the new community of faith solved the issue.

I have longed for years to find and experience the dynamic of the early church community. If you have read Tim Kurtz's book, "**Leaving Church, Becoming Ekklesia**", you understand my reluctance to use the title Church and from this point forward, if I use the word church, it will be to reference the old institution. In Ekklesia I expect to find the absence of walls, disputes, arguments, and divisions over denomina-tional distinctives and differences. How refreshing and naïve would that be. After all, the Ekklesia is still made up of redeemed, sanctified, yet imperfect people.

We do well though, to take a serious look at the model of the early faith movement of the Ekklesia. What did it look like? How did it operate? How does Ekklesia differ from the Church? What is the difference between a "Slave" and a "Servant"? Let's take a serious look at these issues and see if we can gain new insight into our relationship with the Messiah, the Ekklesia and one another.

I'm rather surprised that seemingly none of our Forefathers of Faith have challenged the substitution of the word "church" for Ekklesia. But why should we challenge what we have for centuries believed to be true? I have heard several sermons over my lifetime on Matthew 16:18 and "church" was always used. I have also heard the "church" defined as the Ekklesia but always, only as the "called out ones" or "set apart people" and never the complete meaning, "**the Lord's divine, ruling, governing Council**."

This makes all the difference! It is the difference in having a Berean lifestyle or a lifestyle of dependence on the word being rightly divided in the hands of a few. Could it be a part of centuries old deception of the church? It certainly casts a new paradigm in our identity as a community of faith. We have responsibilities beyond evangelism.

CHAPTER 1

ARE YOU A SLAVE? OR ARE YOU A SERVANT?

I've thought many times it would be fun way to start a class, teaching or a sermon with this question: "How many slaves do we have in attendance today?"

I understand the very word "slave" would excite a lot of people today and hopefully, they would be able to overcome their fight or flight instinct to act on neither. For this reason, let's establish and agree that man oppresses and God frees.

Please hear me out on the topic of Biblical slavery and servanthood. Because I believe that we the Body of Christ, have misrepresented both words: **doulos** and **Ekklesia** – as the Ekklesia (the Lord's divine, ruling, governing Council), we need to set the narrative on these two words.

First, in the New Testament, the Greek word "*doulos*" represents both words. Doulos is the Greek term for both slave and servant. When I discovered that the Greek only has one term, my question was, how do we know when it means "Slave" or "Servant."

Here is one observation. In Luke 22:24-27 (TLV) Jesus instructs his disciples about "greatness." We all can learn from this account as Jesus says, *"The kings of the nations have mastery over them, and those exercising authority over them are called 'benefactors.' But with you, it is not so. Rather, let the one who is greatest among you become like the youngest, and the one who leads like the one who serves. For who is greater, the one who reclines or the one who serves? Is it not the one who reclines? But I am among you as one who serves."*

Notice that Jesus contrasts the world system of "mastery" or some translations say, "lord it over", with greatness in His kingdom. Essentially, all other kingdoms are identified by domination or forced servitude.

Jesus emphatically expresses, *"But with you, it is not so."* This behavior is not to be our lifestyle. In His kingdom, Jesus identifies the one who serves as the "greater" one. So, if you want to be great, "serve."

We not only hear Jesus discuss servanthood, but we see Him demonstrate to us what servanthood looks like. In John 13:4-5, 12-17 (TLV) we are told,

> *"So He (Jesus) gets up from the meal and lays aside His outer garment; and taking a towel, He wrapped it around His waist. Then He pours water into a basin. He began to wash the disciple's feet, drying them with the towel wrapped around him."*

> *"So, after He had washed their feet and put His robe back on and reclined again, He said to them, Do you understand what I have done for you? You call Me Teacher and Master—and*

rightly you say, for I am. So if I, your Master and Teacher, have washed your feet, you also ought to wash each other's feet. I have given you an example—you should do for each other what I have done for you. Amen, amen I tell you; a servant isn't greater than his master, and the one who is sent isn't greater than the one who sent him. If you know these things, you are blessed if you do them!"

It registers with me, that if Jesus needs to tell us to be servants, this lifestyle doesn't come naturally. It seems such a simple concept, yet it is extremely difficult for most of us. What? Wash another person's feet? Have you seen some people's feet? Have you noticed recently the number of advertisements for nail fungus medication?

Many people feel self-conscious about their feet. Others find the thought of someone touching their feet a highly personal experience. If you have never experienced having your feet washed by someone else in the manner Jesus washed feet, you have missed out. Do not be surprised by tears and weeping. Overcome by the demonstration of love exhibited in washing their feet.

We foolishly think that the only kind of slavery in this world, is of the racial variety. There are many more types of "slavery". Many are underground and have been hidden from public view. Some are foisted upon mankind by oppressive political regimes and dictators. Other types are the clandestine work of a spiritual enslaver. They are the dirty secrets of the world system.

Mankind: A common denominator

All types of slavery are characterized by oppression, persecution, ill treatment, repression, suppression, subjection, enslavement, tyranny, exploitation, cruelty, ruthlessness, harshness, brutality, injustice, misery, pain, anguish, maltreatment, and subjugation.

The common denominator amongst these various forms of ill treatment, mankind. All are forms of oppression wielded by man upon man. Some forms are individualized and exercised person to person. Others are institutionalized and wielded by those in control over their subjects, clients, or constituents.

Some of the most egregious demonstrations of tyranny in history were found in an article titled, "***Here are the 10 Most Cruel and Despotic Leaders of the 20th Century***". To make the list, "*there also had to be other less than savory attributes exhibited by these leaders. A penchant for violence, murder, genocidal tendencies, and/or other deviances were prerequisites to make this top ten list.*"

1. **Idi Amin Dada** (In power: 1971-1979) Uganda. He dumped opposition bodies into the Nile river infested with crocodiles.

2. **Pol Pot** (In power: 1975-1979) Cambodia. His methods were starvation, forced labor, torture and executions of an estimated 1.5 million Cambodians.

3. **Joseph Stalin** (In power: 1929-1953) Russia. An

estimated 20 million were executed or perished directly or indirectly under his orders.

4. **Augusto Pinochet** (1973-1990) Chile. He had an estimated 130 thousand arrested and many tortured. Another 3k were executed or removed through forced disappearances.

5. **Mobutu Sese Seko** (1965-1997) Belgian Congo. He later renamed this area, "Zaire". He also gave himself a new name: Mobutu Sese Seko Nkuku Ngbondu Wu Za Sanga ("The all-powerful warrior who, because of his endurance and inflexible will to win, goes from conquest to conquest, leaving fire in his wake"). In other words, destruction was his operative. He also acquired an estimated personal fortune over 5 Billion USD.

6. **Mao Tse Tung** (1949-1976) China. Mao was the first chairman of the Community (Communist) party. He instituted many cultural and social reforms. One of which was the infamous "Great Leap Forward" in 1958. The result was one of the worst manmade famines in history where an estimated 40 million people died of starvation.

7. **Nicolae Ceausescu** (1965-1989) Romania. It is estimated that he had as many as 64 thousand shot and killed. Ceausescu and his wife were executed by firing squad.

8. **Kim Il Sung** (In power 1948-1994) N. Korea. During a three-year period beginning in June 1950, over 2 million Koreans on both sides were killed. N. Korea stayed under Soviet influence while S. Korea stayed under United States stewardship. The war ended in an armistice.

9. **Mengistu Haile Marram** (In power: 1977-1991) Ethiopia. His economic reforms and policies directly contributed to the great famine of the early 1980's which killed an estimated 1.2 million from famine related hunger.

10. **Adolph Hitler** (In power: 1933-1945) Germany. Hitler is the most notorious man on this list and probably best known. He came to power leading the Nazi party. "His vehement anti-Semitism would lead to the Holocaust and his desire to conquer Europe would lead to the beginning of World War II. During the war, his Nazi regime would be responsible for an estimated 19 million civilian and prisoners of war (including those killed in concentration camps)."

The following list is a collection of favorite enslavement tactics imposed upon the people and nations of the world. It is in no way an exhaustive or comprehensive list as man is always in the process of creating more creative ways of enslaving each other.

1. **Economic slavery**: The Bible tells us in Proverbs 22: 7 "The rich rule over the poor, and the borrower is a slave to

the lender." Never have we seen this verse demonstrated in a greater way than today. One of Dave Ramsey's blog posts states: "*debt is dumb—but it still has a choke hold on so many of our friends and family members. Most normal people are just plain broke. They are in debt up to their eyeballs with no hope of help. If you're in debt, you don't have the freedom to use your money the way you want.*"

How bad is it? According to a Pew Charitable Trusts report, 47% of Baby Boomers have mortgage debt, 41% have credit card debt, 13% have school loans, and 36% have car payments.

According to a December 16, 2019 article written by Cameron Huddleston in **Go Banking Rates**, a survey states that 69% of Americans have less than $1K in savings. Americans claim that the cost of living causes them to live paycheck to paycheck. Is this the case or is the demands of our lifestyle that which keeps us from saving?

We must include taxation in this category. For an overview of the history of money, currency, the Federal Reserve, Central Banks, and taxation, please refer to: "The Hidden Secrets of Money" Video series by Mike Maloney. Here's the YouTube link to all the Episodes: https://www.youtube.com/watch?v=DyV0OfU3-FU&list=PLE88E9ICdiphYjJkeeLL2O09eJoC8r7Dc

2. **Sex Trade Slavery**: This form of slavery comes in several varieties. The highest percentage involves females,

and most are very young, however, this category is not exclusive to females.

It involves drugs and lots of money. It is a favorite addiction of the wealthy and affluent. Abhorrent sex is used as an initiation rite to be included into the secret society of the wealthy. Most of us have only seen or been aware of brothels, pornography in all forms (print, DVD, digital), sexualization of advertising, while unaware of the underbelly of pedophilia, the kidnapping and selling of young children, torture and ritual, sacrificial killing. If you are not aware of global sex trafficking or pedophilia rings, please do an internet search.

3. **Drugs**: It has taken over 50 years to obtain legalization of marijuana, but it is now available to the public. Marijuana continues to be the gateway drug to an assortment of available harder drugs.

The legal and illegal drug industry is a financial juggernaut that is global in nature. Drugs are the sustaining economy in some countries and have a pervasive impact on society including cost of recovery programs, crime, theft, prostitution, addiction, suicide, and loss of life is staggering. Here is a link to the government website:
https://www.drugabuse.gov/drug-topics/trends-statistics

4. **Movie/Music Industries**: This is an elite club that elicits immense influence and power over western culture and has spread into vast overseas markets wanting to

emulate western culture. This category warrants an entire book to its own. The pervasive elements of drugs, mysticism, cultic seduction, religious philosophy, mind sciences, psychic exploration, cybernetics, new age, and satanic influence make its brand of programming and mind control epically dangerous.

Do you remember a move titled ***Cabaret*?** If you have never seen this movie, it stars Liza Minelli. A cabaret for those not familiar with the term was a Las Vegas style night club with food, drink, and entertainment. The club participants and entertainment in ***Cabaret*** are effectively mirroring the pre-war lifestyle that led to Germany's fall. The club was a microcosm of the pre-war morality which brought susceptibility to Nazism. In fact, the lifestyle is strikingly similar to the current moral fiber of America.

Could it be the lure and seduction of the arts and entertainment industry that is influencing our acceptance of lifestyles in opposition to Jesus?

5. **Religion**: The master of deception and counterfeit has infiltrated the Vatican, denominations, seminaries, and Christian universities.

Universities like Princeton that used to be Christian based have traveled far from their original roots. Nonprofits that were once Christian base have also forsaken their heritage.

The writers of the epistles warned of false apostles and prophets. Here's what John says, "*Loved ones, do not believe every spirit, but test the spirits to see if they are from God. For many false prophets have gone out into the world. You know the Ruach Elohim by this—every spirit that acknowledges that Messiah Yeshua has come in human flesh is from God, but every spirit that does not acknowledge Yeshua is not from God. This is the spirit of the anti-messiah, which you have heard is coming and* **now is already in the world**." (1 John 4:1-3) TLV.

Did you catch the last line? "*The spirit of anti-messiah...is already in the world.*" When was John writing this? The best scholars point to a A.D. 85-90 as a publishing date. John knew that the spirit of anti-Messiah was already on the earth.

As an example of the existence of the spirit of anti-Messiah over the centuries I believe that this same spirit (along with his lust for power and control) which perhaps used and influenced King James to alter two key concepts: i) the change of the real definition of Ekklesia and insertion of the word "church"; and ii) the use of the lesser word for "*duolos*", replacing the more accurate word "slave" with the word "servant".

These two key concepts have impacted the way Bible scholars and followers of Jesus have viewed the roles of both words in their lives.

What do each of these various forms of slavery have in common? All of them in some way are involved in the occult. In other words, each has a satanically based foundation.

Have you ever noticed the symbols associated with satanic involvement? Have you ever noticed the satanic symbols on your paper money, with the sex trade industry, and satanic symbolism used in movies and video.

I'm not going to go over the various satanic symbols. Just to say, I believe "we" diminished the significance of the symbols and completely disregarded the idea of satanic involvement. There was a line in the movie, The *Usual Suspects*, "*The greatest trick the devil ever pulled was to convince the world that he didn't exist*," uttered by an actor alleged to be involved in satanic activity.

I say that to say this: The spirit of antichrist has been with us for ages. Satanic activity in not new but it is manifesting in more ways than ever, such as on the Internet.

For centuries the phrase, New World Order has been used. This phrase is the English equivalent for the Latin, Novus ordo seclorum. If you haven't been listening to our former Presidents such as George H.W. Bush, they have used the term openly in speeches.

It feels to me that there is a coordinated attack of satanically groomed systems converging onto the scene. All these systems – International Banking, the World Health Organization, the United Nations, ANTIFA, the World Economic Order, the "Global Political Economy" field of study, the World Government Summit, etc. – are conveniently piggy backing on the Covid-19 shutdown and the Black Lives Matter (BLM) civil and social justice unrest.

If you are mesmerized by the local demonstrations of protest for BLM and the deception of the COVID-19 crisis, you are being distracted from the larger global agenda. If you feel that you are currently being oppressed, you haven't seen anything yet. We are about to find out what suppression, domination and slavery is all about.

CHAPTER 2

CHOOSE TODAY WHO YOU WILL SERVE! OR WHO IS YOUR MASTER?

I have already referred to King James. I know that I have riled many who have advocated for the King James Bible as being the "only" Bible they will read.

I only wish that years ago, I had questioned this someone who had a translation of the Bible named after himself. I wish I had questioned an individual, who placed himself as head of the Church of England. Shouldn't that raise some "red flags" for all of us?

Creating a new translation of the Bible sounded like a noble enterprise. Even the way he went about securing the finest translators of his time seemed like a scholarly approach. Men from Oxford, Cambridge and Westminster were selected. The translators weren't paid directly, but received support from their colleges, received promotions or new appointments as they came available. From my research, I believe that the King had an agenda that wasn't noble in nature (please refer to addendums in the back of book). He wanted control and unchallenged supremacy.

Were you aware that while King James was having a new translation created, he was writing two books of his own? He wrote two works about the divine right of Kings *'Basilikan doron'* and *'The True Laws of Free Monarchies*. The first one is a defense of the divine right of kings. The second one is a more practical guide to kingship, written for his son. What King James was establishing was his "supremacy" in being a king and the subsequent right to be the head of the church of England.

When you survey the Wikipedia synopsis of King James tasking the leading seminaries of England to create a new translation, how he contracted the very best of credentialed, scholarly men for this work, it all seems very noble. He put in place a system of documents with notes to the side, to provide checking the work and counter checking amongst the scholars.

But notice that King James had his detractors (Pilgrims), who argued for a Presbytery or a council. King James wanted unchallenged authority as evidenced by crafting his list of guidelines (see Addendum).

I have been in sales over my lifetime. I will never forget a conversation I was privileged to listen in on during a sales call in the mid-nineties. I was working for a telecom company at the time. I introduced the owner and a management associate to a large company about a certain product.

After the sales meeting with this client, we were driving back to corporate headquarters and he instructed the manager to offer to draft an RFP (request for proposal) for this company. He explained that this was the process that all companies offered and it happened all the time. Notice that if you can write the requirements for the RFP, you have a significant leg up on your competition. You end up using the standards for the results which your equipment can deliver.

King James did something like this. He maintained control by installing requirements that kept him in power as the head of the church.

I believe he did this in at least two ways. The first was the use of the word "church" rather than "Ekklesia" which Tim Kurtz effectively writes about in his book, ***Leaving Church, Becoming Ekklesia***. Secondly, I believe he also chose to have the scholars use the word "servant" in place of "slave" so as not to disparage the word, "slave" due to slavery being the main economic means of England at that time.

CHAPTER 3

SELF-IDENTIFIED AS SLAVES

I believe that by going to the Bible, the Bible can and does interpret itself.

Let's look at the one chapter that I believe gives us insight into the issue of slavery. In Romans 6 (TLV), Paul addresses the topic of sin and death and the transitory nature of redemption. Listen to the language he uses in verse 8, *"Now if we have died with Messiah, we believe that we shall also live with Him. We know that Messiah, having been raised from the dead, no longer dies; death no longer is master over Him"*.

Paul continues in verse 14 (bold emphasis mine),

*"For sin shall not be master over you, for you are not under law but under grace. ... **Do you not know that to whatever you yield yourselves as slaves for obedience, you are slaves to what you obey**—whether to sin resulting in death, or to obedience resulting in righteousness? But thanks be to God that though you were slaves of sin, you wholeheartedly obeyed the form of teaching under which you were placed; and*

after you were set free from sin, you became enslaved to righteousness. I speak in human terms because of the weakness of your flesh. For just as you yielded your body parts as slaves to uncleanness and lawlessness, leading to more lawlessness, so now yield your body parts as slaves to righteousness resulting in holiness. For when you were slaves of sin, you were free with regard to righteousness. So then, what outcome did you have that you are now ashamed of? For the end of those things is death. But no, having been set free from sin and having become enslaved to God, you have your fruit resulting in holiness. And the outcome is eternal life. For sin's payment is death, but God's gracious gift is eternal life in Messiah Yeshua our Lord." (emphasis mine)

Do you see? We once were slaves of darkness, sin, evil, lawlessness, and uncleanness but now, we are slaves of righteousness, holiness, and light. We once were slaves of our father the devil, but now we are slaves of Jesus.

I believe with all my heart and being, that the apostles who wrote the New Testament self-identified as **bond slaves** of Jesus, *not* bond servants.

Who in the Bible are identified as bond slaves of Jesus? (How many names can you list without looking?

1. **Epaphras** - Colossians 1:7; 4:12 is called by Paul, "a bond-slave of Jesus Christ in Colossians 4: 12.
2. **James** - James 1:1 the half-brother of Jesus self-addresses himself as "a bond-slave of God and of the

Lord Jesus Christ."

3. **John** - Revelation 1:1; Acts 4:29 self-addresses in Revelation 1:1 as a "bond-slave", after he reveals to us the purpose of the book of Revelation. *"The Revelation of Jesus Christ, which God gave Him to show to His bond-slaves, the things which must shortly take place; and He sent and communicated it by His angel to His bond-slave John".*

   Typically, John doesn't identify himself other than saying, the apostle that Jesus loved. Here he says, this is the message given to Jesus to communicate to His "bonded", "bought with a price of His own shed blood", the future things that will come were revealed by an angel to John.

4. **Jude** - Jude 1:1 self-address as *"a bond-slave of Jesus Christ."*

5. **Mary** - Luke 1:38,48 (NASB) (mother of Jesus) Mary responds to the news given her by Gabriel, the angel sent by God to deliver a message of "favor with God" (1:30) about her being chosen to be the instrument of God to birth Jesus. Mary replies by saying, *"Behold, the bond-slave of the Lord; be it done to me according to your word."* Then, just a few verses further in the text, Mary is praising God and proclaims (vs. 46-48b), 46 "My soul exalts the Lord, 47 "And my spirit has rejoiced in God my Savior. 48 "For He has had regard for the humble state of His bond-slave." What a profound proclamation by a young woman unto the Sovereign!

6. **Moses** - Revelation 15:3 "the servant of God"
7. **Paul** - Galatians 1:10; Titus 1:1; Acts 16:17 (us?); Philippians 1:1; Romans 1:1 self identifies as a bondservant of Christ Jesus in several epistles but first in Romans 1:1 *"Paul, a bond-slave of Christ Jesus…"*. Galatians 1:10 Paul says something interesting, *"If I were still trying to please men, I would not be a bond-slave of Christ."* In Titus 1:1, Paul again self-addresses himself as "a bond-slave of God, and an apostle of Jesus Christ." In 2 Corinthians 4:5, Paul states, *"For we do not preach ourselves but Christ Jesus as Lord, and ourselves as your bond-slave for Jesus' sake."*
8. **Peter** - 2 Peter 2:1; Acts 4:29 self-addresses in 2 Peter 1:1 as *"a bond-slave and apostle of Jesus Christ."*
9. **Simeon** - Luke 2:29 the Priest that has prayed that he might see the consolation of Israel before he dies. Jesus has been brought to the temple to be dedicated by Simeon and in this whole process, Simeon self-proclaims as being a "bond-slave" of God.
10. **Timothy** - Philippians 1:1 (see #12)
11. **Tychicus** - Colossians 4:7 "trustworthy servant and fellow slave to the Lord"
12. **Paul & Timothy** - Philippians 1:1 Paul addresses both Timothy and himself as "bond-slaves of Messiah Yeshua"

Note: The TLV sometimes uses that term "emissaries" instead of servant or slave

What are the Biblical qualifications of a bond-slave? (2 Timothy 2:24)

1. Must not be quarrelsome.
2. Must be kind to all; able to teach; patient when wronged; gentleness (when) correcting those who are in opposition; uses his bond-slave as a covering for good (God) 1 Peter 2:16.

Why do I prefer the term bond-slave rather than bond-servant?

What is the difference between a servant and a slave?

A servant is defined as "a devoted and helpful follower or supporter". They retain free will and can leave or go home whenever they want to. A slave is "a person who is the legal property of another and serves a Master.

The key difference is freedom and rights. Understand that all the people on our list voluntarily proclaimed (what I am calling "self-identified") themselves as "bond-slaves" of Jesus. He didn't force them to be His slaves, but they were compelled by love and conviction to willingly die for the One who died for them.

Scriptural support for considering a lifestyle change from servant to bond-slave:

1. Jesus, the greatest bond-slave, is our example: Philippians 2: 1-11 (key 5-7) "*Have this attitude in yourselves which was in Christ Jesus, who, although He existed*

in the form of God, did not regard equality with God a thing to be grasped, but emptied Himself, taking the form of a bond-slave, and being made in the likeness of men."

2. Jesus' prayer in the Garden of Gethsemane: Luke 22: 42; Matthew 26:39 *"My Father, if it is possible, let this cup pass from Me; yet not as I will, but as Thou wilt."* This prayer is not spoken by a servant with rights but a bond-slave that is yielding all rights in submission to the will of God.

3. Jesus example on the cross: Luke 23:34 *"Father, forgive them; for they do not know what they are doing."* It was Jesus' love that kept Him on the cross and kept Him from calling ten thousand angels. Luke 23:46 *"Father, into Thy hands I commit My Spirit."* Jesus had completed His mission, sent by God. This was true love and humility of Divinity in the flesh.

What Greater Compliment

We are called to "Be holy" (1 Peter 1:16); we are called to "be perfect" (Matthew 5:48). Just as Jesus did what He saw the Father doing (John 5:19), so also we should strive to do what we see Jesus doing. He calls each of us to "follow Him." Then He teaches us all to be disciples, apostles, pastors, teachers, evangelists, ambassadors through His Word, through the Spirit and through the various callings that I just listed.

We are called to be like Jesus. What greater compliment could we give our Master than to yield ourselves like Paul, Timothy, John, Mary, Peter, and the host of others as a bond-slave of Jesus?

1 Corinthians 6:19-20 *"Or do you not know that your body is a temple of the Holy Spirit who is in you, whom you have from God, and that you are not your own? For you have been bought with a price: (the blood of Jesus purchased our pardon on Calvary) therefore glorify God in your body."*

Ephesians 6:9 *"And, masters (earthly), do the same things to them (your slaves), and give up threatening, knowing that both their Master (God) and yours is in heaven, and there is not partiality with Him."*

Colossians 4:1 *"Masters, grant to your slaves justice and fairness, knowing that you too have a Master in heaven."*

2 Timothy 2:21 *"Therefore, if a man cleanses himself from these things, he will be a vessel for honor, sanctified, useful to the Master, prepared for every good work."*

Why would Paul use the terminology "Master" (capitalized) if that weren't the relationship that God desires? Paul used "Master" because again, he saw himself as a bond-slave to Jesus and God and not just a servant. He and the others on the list were compelled to serve Jesus with all the convictions of their heart, mind, soul and strength (Deut. 6:5; Matt. 22:37; Mk 12:30; Lk 10:27).

Horizontal and Vertical

Here is an additional observation. The use of "servant" and "slave" has a vertical and horizontal dimension. When Jesus said that He does only what He sees the Father doing and tells us He came to serve people, it makes sense that we are to do likewise. We are to serve people (horizontal) and be both slave and servant to God (vertical). Jesus frees while the enemy suppresses. Jesus frees while fallen people suppress.

We were never meant to be slaves of sin, money, wealth, food, to lust, government, sex, man or woman, our eyes, mind, or heart. Our heart was meant for God. We are to love Him with all our heart, mind and soul, and our neighbor as ourselves. When God has our heart, he has all of us. "For where your treasure is, there will your heart be also (Matt. 6:21)." TLV

What you value most, is where your heart will be focused. It is where your affections will reside. Are you captivated with Jesus? Does God have your "whole heart"? This is what He requires!

CHAPTER 4

BUT WHAT ABOUT...?

I can already hear the arguments to the transition between servant and slave. Probably the biggest argument will come from those citing Galatians 3: 28-29 *"There is neither Jew nor Greek, there is neither slave nor free, there is neither male nor female—for you are all one in Messiah Yeshua. And if you belong to Messiah, then you are Abraham's seed—heirs according to the promise."*

I have heard this text interpreted as a case for freedoms for several arguments in church polity. My initial question that I would offer: Is Paul talking in a spiritual context or a physical context?

Can we all agree that Paul is speaking in a spiritual context? While we agree that we are a new creation positionally before God, we don't instantly, while on earth lose or shed our physical identity. We are still male and female, we are still identified ethnically, and we may be a slave or free in the world system.

Kingdom Theology

Jesus was speaking about His kingdom. Here are two examples of kingdom thought. In John 18 Jesus is being interrogated by Pilate, *"Are you the King of the Jews?"* His response, *"My kingdom is not of this world. If My kingdom were of this world, then My servants would be fighting so that I wouldn't be handed over to the Judean leaders. But as it is, My kingdom is not from here."* So Pilate said to Him, *"Are you a king, then?"* Yeshua answered, *"You say that I am a king. For this reason I came into the world, so that I might testify to the truth. Everyone who is of the truth hears My voice."* Pilate said to Him, *"What is truth?"*

In actuality, Truth was standing right before him!

Jesus established with Pilate that His kingdom was not here on earth (yet!). This statement told Pilate: "I am not a threat to you. Do you see My servants fighting for Me?" Remember, Jesus at his arrest told Peter to put the sword away and He healed the servant of a centurion. This account is captured in all four gospels (Matthew 26:51, Mark 14:47, Luke 22:50–51, and John 18:10–11). Jesus was not leading an insurrection; His purpose was to die for all mankind.

In the letter to Philemon, Paul gives us a real-life example of a slave (Onesimus) and master (Philemon) relationship. Apparently, Onesimus robbed his master and in his flight to Rome, providentially crossed paths with Paul.

Easton's Bible Dictionary share's a narrative about Onesimus this way: Onesimus – *"useful, a slave who, after robbing his master Philemon (q.v.) at Colosse, fled to Rome, where he was converted by the apostle Paul, who sent him back to his master with the epistle which bears his name. In it he beseeches Philemon to receive his slave as a 'faithful and beloved brother.' Paul offers to pay to Philemon anything his slave had taken, and to bear the wrong he had done him. He was accompanied on his return by Tychicus, the bearer of the Epistle to the Colossians."*

I find it interesting that Paul uses "useful" in his description of Onesimus (his name literally means useful or helpful) and Paul once again, self-describes as a "spiritual father while in chains" to Onesimus. He led Onesimus to Jesus while he was on the run. Onesimus became born again and was freed spiritually, but doing the right thing, Paul was returning him to Philemon.

We can be assured that Onesimus served Philemon like he never had before, with Jesus now in his heart. He became useful to both Paul and Philemon.

It was the internal transformation within Saul that produced a Paul and the same with Onesimus. It is all about the heart and relationship. This is another scriptural resource to underscore this topic.

A Slave Lifestyle

In a part of scripture that you would not anticipate finding support for a slave lifestyle, we find this counsel in 1 Corinthians 7: 10-14 (TLV)

"Only, as the Lord has assigned to each one, as God has called each, let him walk in this way. I give this rule in all of Messiah's communities." "Were you called as a slave? Don't let that bother you—but if indeed you can become free, make the most of the opportunity. For the one who was called in the Lord as a slave is the Lord's freedman. Likewise the one who was called while free is Messiah's slave. You were bought with a price; do not become slaves of men. Brothers and sisters, let each one—in whatever way he was called—remain that way with God."

Why would Paul advocate for all of us to stay with the relationship, the lifestyle that God found us, when He called us if he didn't mean it? His mission was not to change our external conditions. He sought to change us from the inside out.

If our relationship with God is not right, it will not be right with our fellow man. Why? Because we are on the throne. Only He can transform us, change us.

Have you heard the joke about how many therapists it takes to change a lightbulb? Answer: Only 1! But the lightbulb has got to want to change!

We too, must want to change to be transformed. Even though He may motivate you to desire to change, He won't violate your will. He is longsuffering, thankfully. But He does have a limit, a boundary that can be reached. Romans 1: 24-32 provides us with full gravity of resisting His will.

The question that begs to be asked is: "***Who owns you?***"

Words were penned in 1865 by Elvina M. Hall as she sat listening to a sermon. Little did she know that the organist at her church had written a tune that fit perfectly with her words.

As the pastor's prayer continued, Mrs. Hall took up her hymn book, and turning to a blank page inside the cover, she began to write.

Afterward, she presented the pastor with some simple lines of poetry–not likely telling him when they were written! Glancing at them, the pastor was reminded of something that had happened just that week.

The church organist, John Grape (1835-1915) had composed a new hymn-tune, with *no lyrics* in mind. He passed it on to Pastor Schrick, suggesting they might find a use for it in future.

Stepping into his study, the pastor laid Mrs. Hall's poem next to the lines of music. To his surprise, he saw they fit one another like hand in glove. "Indeed, God works in mysterious ways!" he thought. Little did he know! To this day, the lyrics and tune have been partners ever since, in the hymn, "Jesus Paid It All"!!

Jesus Paid It All

I hear the Savior say, thy strength indeed is small
Child of weakness, watch and pray, find in me thine all in all

'Cause Jesus paid it all, All to him I owe
Sin had left a crimson stain, he washed it white as snow
Lord, now indeed I find thy power and thine alone
Can change the leper's spots and melt the heart of stone

'Cause Jesus paid it all, All to him I owe
My sin had left this crimson stain, he washed it white as snow
It's washed away, all my sin
And all my shame
And when before the throne I stand in him complete
"Jesus died my soul to save" my lips shall still repeat

Jesus paid it all, All to him I owe
(Sin had left a crimson stain, he washed it white as snow)
(He washed it white as snow)

CHAPTER 5

SIMPLE STORIES, PROFOUND TRUTHS

"For this reason I speak to them in parables, because seeing they do not see, and hearing they do not hear, nor do they understand." Matthew 13:13 TLV

I would be remiss not to acknowledge the simple stories and profound truths that we call the "parables of Jesus." They are contained in the gospels of Matthew, Mark and Luke and were Jesus' way to disguise wisdom that was not meant to be understood by everyone.

Jesus reveals his purpose in Matthew 13 when He is asked by His disciples, *"Why do You speak to them in parables?"* And He replied to them, *"To you has been given to know the secrets of the kingdom of heaven, but to them it has not been given."*

The secrets of the kingdom are not meant for everyone's understanding, but only those who are of His kingdom. Even then, the disciples needed clarification. I believe that their eyes, hearts, and minds had *not yet* been opened to receive the illuminating work of the Holy Spirit.

The Holy Spirit had not yet been sent. The "power of Pentecost" had not yet arrived and manifested in the lives of Jesus followers.

In many of the parables Jesus used language like, "Master, servant and slave." He was using the method of simple storytelling to illustrate profound moral or spiritual truths. He also used real life examples that were easily relatable. While we may get the comparison to earthly relationships, we don't easily make the connection to spiritual things.

Here is an example of a direct correlation found in John 8: 34, *"Amen, amen I tell you, everyone who sins is a slave to sin."* Do we quickly accept the connection spiritually to being a "slave" to sin, or the act of becoming enslaved to sin?

The light didn't come on till much later in my life and journey with Christ. You see, I have been a "Pharisee" for many years. Not only did I not recognize my enslavement to sin, but instead, feeling self-righteous about it.

The issue of sin and its various forms is expansive and pervasive. Not only do we have sins of commission and omission, sins of our body, mind, eyes and tongue, we are told in scripture that to know what to do and not do it is sin! (see James 4:17)

Being a bond-slave of Jesus is both an internal and external expression of one's will. It is the application of

Romans 12: 1, where Paul "urges" us to present your body and entire being (lay yourself on the altar) as a "living sacrifice". Our rights at that point are terminated, dead.

I wish I could say that I have achieved total and complete surrender and death of self. I believe this process is a lifetime of putting our "selves" (willfully) back on the altar.

I heard a pastor once preach on this passage and he testified to his "self" crawling off of the altar. The apostle Paul acknowledged his needing to "die daily." (see 1 Cor. 15:31 Please note, if you want a succinct theological accounting of Jesus' death, burial, resurrection, ascension, and His glorious return, 1 Corinthians 15 is the chapter to read!) If Paul needed to "die daily", how much more must we do the same?!

Salvation is for everyone but not all will choose to follow Jesus. Slavery is not for every follower of Jesus because it requires a cost.

One day, a rich young ruler came to Jesus and posed a question, "*What must I do to inherit eternal life?*" After Jesus replied, the response of the rich young ruler, "*He went away grieving, for he had much property.*"

Correspondingly, the apostles mentioned that they had left "everything" to follow Jesus. The "everything" included more than accumulated financial wealth. It included mothers, wives, children, family, houses, and lands. (see Matt. 19:16-30; Mk. 10:17-31; Luke 18:18-30)

The Reward of the Bond-slave

Many of us have worked for many years for a pension that today, is looking like it may not be there for us upon retirement.

Jesus gave his apostles some insight into His kingdom and its reward system in Luke 18: 29-30 (TLV), "*Amen, I tell you, there is no one who has left house or wife or brothers or parents or children, for the sake of the kingdom of God, who will not receive many times as much in this age, and the (olam ha-ba), eternal life.*"

This is a pension that is promised, secure and no man will be able to take it away from us. I believe this reward is specifically for those who are lifestyle bond-slaves of Jesus.

There is an additional reward to those who embrace this attitude and aspire to serving God as a bond-slave.

It is found in the book of Revelation and begins in chapter 11:18 "*And the nations were enraged, and Thy wrath came, and the time came for the dead to be judged, and the time to give their reward to Thy bond-servants the prophets and to the saints and to those who fear Thy name, the small and the great and to destroy those who destroy the earth.*"

19:1-2 "*After these things I heard, as it were, a loud voice of a great multitude in heaven, saying, Hallelujah! Salvation and glory and power belong to our God; Because His Judgments Are True And Righteous; for He has judged the great harlot who was corrupting the earth with her immorality, and He Has Avenged The Blood Of His Bond-Slaves On Her.*"

22:3 *"And there shall no longer be any curse; and the throne of God and of the Lamb shall be in it, and His bond-slaves shall serve Him; and they shall see His face, and His name shall be on their foreheads. And there shall no longer be any night; and they shall not have need of the light of a lamp nor the light of the sun, because the Lord God shall illumine them; and they shall reign forever and ever. And he (the angel of God) said to me, "These words are faithful and true"; and the Lord, the God of the spirits of the prophets, sent His angel to show to His bond-slaves the things which must shortly take place."* NASB (I've taken the liberty to change to bond-slaves)

It is incredibly clear that the bond-slaves of Jesus have a very special place in the New Jerusalem and are rewarded by being front and center in providing service and worship to Jesus face to face! What a glorious picture that is!

Greater Things, do you receive it?

For those who ascribe to self-identify as a bond-slave of Jesus, I want to encourage you to count the cost, and consider the rewards. The apostle Paul gives us an overview of the perils he faced in spreading the gospel in 2 Cor. 11: 16-33.

Jesus gives us an inspirational message in John 14: 12-14 (TLV) where He says, *"Amen, amen I tell you, he who puts his trust in Me, the works that I do he will do; and greater than these he will do, because I am going to the Father. And whatever you ask in*

My name, that I will do, so that the Father may be glorified in the Son. If you ask Me anything in My name, I will do it."

I want to experience in my life and see in the lives of other bond-slaves, the greater works and miracles – greater than those that Jesus did. This is a promise and proclamation of Jesus that I claim today for all who would self-identify as Jesus bond-slaves.

He said for those "who put or place wholly" their trust in HIM, they would do *greater works* than HE did! These are amazing, powerful words that Jesus didn't speak lightly.

He proclaimed these words with the full authority of heaven! He is telling us, "Thus says the LORD, it will be so!"

Will we trust Jesus at His word?

Glory! I am so excited to begin seeing in my life and in the lives of fellow bond-slaves of Jesus, the living out of these "greater works" in the power and authority of Jesus!

CHAPTER 6

CONFORMED TO HIS IMAGE

The apostle Paul wrote a letter to the community in Philippi from prison. The letter emphatically calls the followers of Jesus to think a certain way.

Listen to what Paul says, *"Only live your lives in a manner worthy of the Good News of the Messiah. Then, whether I come and see you or I am absent, I may hear of you that you are standing firm in one spirit—striving side by side with one mind for the faith of the Good News and not being frightened in any way by your opponents. For them this is a sign of destruction, but for you salvation—and that from God. For to you was granted for Messiah's sake not only to trust in Him, but also to suffer for His sake—experiencing the same struggle you saw in me and now you are hearing in me."* Philippians 1:27-30 TLV

Paul continues in Philippians 2:5-11 TLV:

"Have this attitude in yourselves, which also was in Messiah Yeshua, Who, though existing in the form of God, did not consider being equal to God a thing to be grasped. But He

> *emptied Himself— **taking on the form of a slave**, becoming the likeness of men and being found in appearance as a man. He humbled Himself— becoming obedient to the point of death, even death on a cross. For this reason God highly exalted Him and gave Him the name that is above every name, that at the name of Yeshua every knee should bow, in heaven and on the earth and under the earth, and every tongue profess that Yeshua the Messiah is Lord to the glory of God the Father."* (emphasis mine)

When Jesus went to the cross He submitted to the Father. Remember His prayer in the garden of Gethsemane? "*Not as I will, but as You will*" TLV (Matt. 26:39; Mark 14:36; Luke 22:42).

Jesus emptied Himself of His own will. Taking the form of a "slave." Notice, it does not say "bond-slave." Why? Because He wasn't being purchased. He was doing the purchasing!

The online definition for a bond: "*an agreement with legal force.*" Also, "*an accounting bond is a written agreement or contract between an issuer and the holder that requires the issuer to pay the holder the bond's par value or face value plus the stated amount of interest.*"

In Christ's death on the cross, He paid for our sin with His blood! Therefore, I contend that the word "bond" does not belong with the word "servant". We pay servants, but we *don't* purchase them. We purchase "slaves." It is an oxymoron to attach the word "bond" to the word "servant".

Servant	Slave
Payment for service	Owned
Lifestyle of service	Lifestyle of servitude
May work a shift	At a master's beck & call 24/7
Has Rights	No Rights
Can leave worksite	Not free to come and go
May Own Property	Is Owned, No Individual Rights

Compelled!

The example of Jesus establishes that if we want to be like Him, we, too, take on the form of a *slave*. It was this attitude that drove the apostles to receive a martyr's death for all except John.

These men had lived and eaten with Jesus. They had observed the miracles He performed. They had observed His resurrection and ascension into Heaven. And most powerfully, they had experienced receiving the Ruach ha-Kodesh, the Holy Spirit!

They were compelled to live for Him who died for them! That is why Paul endured hardship in labors, beatings, five times forty lashes save one, stoning, shipwreck, danger from rivers, robbers, countrymen, Gentiles, in cities, in the desert, among false brothers, sleepless nights, hunger and thirst, in cold and exposure. (2 Cor. 11:21-33)

It was the Lord who spoke to Ananias, *"Go (to Saul), for he is a choice instrument to carry My name before nations and kings and Bnei-Yisrel. For I will show him how much he must suffer for My name's sake."* Acts 9: 15-16 TLV

Prophetically, Ananias was told what Paul later professed. Yet Paul was not deterred, but rather compelled to proclaim the gospel. It is my conviction a servant would not have persevered the hardship Paul endured. Paul self-identified as a bond-slave of Jesus Christ.

Identification with Jesus!

Perhaps Paul's greatest statement of identification with Jesus is found in Galatians 2:19-20 TLV, *"I have been crucified with Messiah; and it is no longer I who live, but Messiah lives in Me."*

It is an honor for the follower of Jesus to live a lifestyle of servitude. It is a process of being born again, identifying with Jesus' death, burial (redemption) and resurrection (eternal destiny).

In the process of living out our salvation and progress in the faith (sanctification, living holy, yielded lives, and transformation), we more fully realize who we are and whose we are, becoming conformed to His image.

This is a lifetime process resulting in eternal living with Jesus.

CHAPTER 7

OPEN YOUR EYES!

I want to take a moment to make some observations about the world's historical systemic oppression.

If we could stand back and take a drone's eye view of the entirety of history with the list of oppressive leaders over the many centuries and the global list of types of slavery, what observations could we make? What common threads are weaved into each of their stories?

Common to man: It is already in the DNA

First, we must acknowledge that **no one culture has a monopoly on evil**. Evil has been a common denominator since the fall of mankind.

We didn't start out this way, but sin entered the picture and has haunted mankind ever since. Can we accept how God sees us? It was wickedness that prompted God to use a flood for a do-over. It was God who established a covenant with man not to do that again by instituting a sign in the sky called a "rainbow".

The rainbow was given by God with a purpose and a meaning. In the grand theme of "good and evil", God creates and the evil one, Satan (the deceiver), perpetuates his folly of "kill, steal, and destroy."

By stealing, we could say that Satan takes and counterfeits or renames what God has named for his purposes. An example in our culture would be the rainbow. Most people today probably do not know that God gave and purposed the rainbow centuries ago. (see Gen. 9:8-19)

It is an easy thing to embrace that man (singularly) is good. However, God knows the heart and man looks only at the outward appearance.

We cannot see the internal thoughts of the mind and feelings of the heart like He can. This is what God says about man. *"Then Adonai saw that the wickedness of humankind was great on the earth, and that every inclination of the thoughts of their heart was only evil all the time."* Genesis 6:5 TLV

Jesus' teaching about man's heart is further embellished in Matthew 15:19 NIV *"For out of the heart come evil thoughts, murder, adultery, sexual immorality, theft, false witness, and slander."*

John 4:3b TLV *"This is the spirit of anti-messiah, which you have heard is coming and now is already in the world."*

Secondly, in continuing our fly-over, we notice a common thread of satanic influence and sometimes downright occultic participation by man. I'll give you several examples.

Biblically, there is much to say about involvement with the occultic. In Deuteronomy 18:10-11 (TLV) we see one of the more all-encompassing examples of what is offensive to God. *"There must not be found among you anyone who makes his son or daughter pass through the fire, or a fortune-teller, soothsayer, omen reader or sorcerer, or one who cast spells, or a medium, a spiritist, or one who calls up the dead."*

This is *not* an exhaustive list but it helps to show the pervasive nature of man's involvements.

For decades horoscopes have been fashionable and even believers would feign innocence and sneak a peak in the newspaper.

We also have an example of a biblical figure – a king, who consults a medium. In 1 Samuel 28, Saul is king over Israel and is facing a battle with the Philistines. Samuel had died and God had not answered Saul "neither by dreams, nor by Urim or prophets." (vs. 6) So, he is told that there is a medium nearby in Endor and he disguises himself, "puts on other clothes" and heads out along with two other men for their destination.

We are told that they arrive in the night. Darkness aids Saul in not being recognized initially, and he approaches the female medium. Saul wants her to conjure up a specific spirit for him and inquires if she would comply. She is initially reticent as she knows that Saul has suppressed or "cut off" the land of this practice. Saul assures her with a vow before God that no punishment would come on her for this thing. So, she proceeds to conjure up the spirit of Samuel.

But, when she sees Samuel, she screams and realizes she has been duped. She recognizes King Saul and is fearful for her life. Saul assures her of her safety and asks her what she sees? "*I see a godlike being coming up from the earth.*" What does he look like? "*An old man is coming up, and he is wrapped with a robe*," she said. Saul knew that it was Samuel, "*so he bowed down and prostrated himself with his face to the ground. Samuel asked Saul, "Why have you disturbed me by bringing me up?" "I'm in great distress*," Saul answered. "*The Philistines are waging war against me, and God has turned away from me—He doesn't answer me anymore, whether by prophets or by dreams. So I called you up to tell me what I should do.*" Samuels short answer..."*Adonai (God) has torn the kingship out of your hand and has given it to another fellow, to David. Since you did not obey the voice of Adonai and did not execute His fierce wrath on Amalek, so Adonai has done this to you today. Moreover, Adonai will also give the Israelites who are with you into the hand of the Philistines. Tomorrow you and your sons will be with me!*" (1 Samuel 28:13-19 (TLV)

What had Saul done wrong? He went to a medium intentionally violating God's command. We are to have nothing to do with any spirit, save God. There are two spirit worlds warring for your soul.

Satan was an angel, who fell when he wanted to usurp God's power and position. When this happened, he took a third of the angelic host with him (Revelation 12: 7-10).

God is a jealous God. He desires to have an exclusive Lordship-relationship with you. (See Exodus 20: 3-5)

We have the DNA of our Father

Further evidence is found in John 8:44-47 (TLV). Jesus is telling his Hebrew audience, "*You are of your father the devil, and you want to do the desires of your father. He was a murderer from the beginning and does not stand in the truth, because there is not truth in him. Whenever he speaks lies, he is just being himself—for he is a liar and the father of lies.*" Jesus continues, "*He who belongs to God hears the words of God. The reason you don't hear is because you do not belong to God*" (vs.47).

Most if not all the world systems I mentioned openly flaunt their association with Satanic symbols and gestures. The lyrics of many of our popular music forms have satanic references. This should not surprise us, especially the household of faith. Paul creates a vivid picture in Romans 1: 18-32. There is too much to unpack in this passage, but he captures the depravity of man without God. In fact, his commentary is about man that "intentionally" disregards what man can see around him that points to a divine creator.

Here are Paul's concluding remarks: "*And just as they did not see fit to recognize God, God gave them over to a depraved mind, to do what is not fitting. They became filled with all unrighteousness, wickedness, greed, evil. They are full of envy, murder, strife, deceit, malice. They are gossips, slanders, God-haters, insolent, haughty, boastful, inventors of evil, disobedient to parents. They are foolish, faithless, heartless, ruthless. Though they know God's righteous decree—that those who practice such things deserve death—they not only do them but also approve of others who practice the same."*

Like Father like Son

There used to be a statement that people would utter, "like father, like son." Or "the apple doesn't fall far from the tree." Or "a chip off the old block." I have discovered that just as proverbs are true in the physical world, they are true in the spiritual world.

I ask you, what do you see manifest in actions and rhetoric of the rioters, looters anarchists, schemers, politicians, religious leaders, sports icons, Hollywood actors/actresses, mega-billionaires, and tech trillionaires?

Here is my answer to everyone contained in three Biblical passages.

Proverbs 21:1 TLV *"A kings heart is like a stream of water in the hand of Adonai, He directs it wherever He wants."*

Daniel 2:20-23 TLV *"Blessed be the Name of God forever and ever, for wisdom and might are His. He changes times and seasons. He removes kings and installs kings. He gives wisdom to the wise and knowledge to the discerning. He reveals deep and hidden things. He knows what lies in darkness and light dwells with Him. To You, O God of my fathers, I give thanks and praise! For You gave me wisdom and power. You have made known to m what we asked You.*

You revealed to us the word of the king." (Daniels prayer to God after receiving the mystery of the kings' vision)

Romans 15: 1b *"For there is no authority except from God, and those that exist are put in place by God."*

We can argue all we want amongst ourselves. And we can wrestle with God about all kinds of issues. But we will lose just like Jacob and perhaps come out with more than a limp. God is in control. He can use anything, even a virus, to His advantage!

Conclusion: Even On My Slaves

You tell me. Was Paul, Timothy, James, Peter and all the others claiming they were "slaves" or "servants" of Messiah Yeshua? While I believe there is an element of both in these men's lives and in Mary's, the mother of Jesus, each of them lived a bold, dynamic life, powered by the Holy Spirit and fueled by a zeal to live for Him who died for them, for you, for me, and for all mankind.

If just a servant, they would have failed.

If just a servant, they would have failed. This was the transition in Peter's life. He confessed, "You are the Messiah, the Son of the living God", mere verses before Jesus declares, *"I also tell you that you are Peter, and upon this rock I will build My community (Ekklesia); and the gates of Sheol will not overpower it."* Then, Peter denies Jesus, watches His death, observes an empty tomb and sees the resurrected Messiah at the Sea of Galilee, hauls in a net full of fish, is asked if he loves Yeshua, is commanded to "feed My sheep", is told to "Follow Him", told by Yeshua to "stay in the city until you are clothed with power from on high"(Luke 24:49 TLV), watches Yeshua ascend into Heaven (Luke 24:51 TLV), received the promise of Acts 1:8 "But you will receive power when the Ruach ha-Kodesh has come upon you; and you will be My witnesses in Jerusalem, and through all Judah, and Samaria, and to the end of the earth."

I want to conclude with one last scripture passage. It is recorded in Acts 2 (TLV) that this same Peter who had stumbled and bumbled his path with Yeshua, now stood with the "eleven" and with power and boldness addressed the assembled crowd on the day of Pentecost. Peter quoted the prophet Joel.

> "And it shall be in the last days, says God,
> That I shall pour out My Ruach on all flesh,
> Your sons and your daughters
> Shall prophesy,
> Your young men shall see visions,
> And your old men shall dream dreams.
> **Even on My slaves**, male and female,
> I will pour out my Ruach in those days,
> And they shall prophesy.
> And I will give wonders in the sky above

> And signs on the earth beneath--
> Blood, and fire, and smoky vapor,
> The sun shall be turned to darkness
> And the moon to blood
> Before the great and glorious
> Day of Adonai comes.
> And it shall be that everyone who calls
> On the name of Adonai
> Shall be saved."
> (emphasis mine)

Did you catch that? "Even on My slaves!

I consider myself a "bond-slave" of Jesus! I hope the testimonies of the apostles and writers of the New Testament have transformed your identity with Jesus.

I believe He is asking us the same questions He asked Peter. I believe He is telling us to "follow Him", just like Peter. We owe Him our lives for dying for us. Truly, Jesus paid it all! All to Him I owe!

CHAPTER 8

A SEVEN DAY DEVOTIONAL

A Seven-Day Bible Study Investigating the Identity of the Community of Faith as Ekklesia and Bond Slaves of Jesus

Seven Hard hitting Issues surrounding the terms "Church", "Ekklesia", "Servant" and "Bond-Slave". We must determine and declare our identity in Christ!

Day 1: On This Rock

Biblical text: Matthew 16: 17-19 TLV Yeshua said to him, *"Blessed are you, Simon son of Jonah, because flesh and blood did not reveal this to you, but My Father who is in heaven! And I also tell you that you are Peter, and upon this rock I will build My community; and the gates of Sheol will not overpower it. I will give you the keys of the kingdom of heaven. Whatever you forbid on earth will have been forbidden in heaven and what you permit on earth will have been permitted in heaven."*

What word did Jesus use in this passage? "Church" or "Ekklesia"? (Please refer to the Addendum in the back of this book and do your own research.)

What is the full definition of the word "Ekklesia"? I have heard pastors use the word "Church" and "Ekklesia" synonymously. Are they the same? If they are not the same, then do they have the same "authority?"

Please write out an application. (For example, write a statement such as: Knowing this information, God, I will do this from now on). This is what James 1: 22-25 calls being "a doer of the word and not a hearer only."

Please prayerfully consider the implications of today's study. Study never comes without its struggles in processing the new information we have heard. None of us wants to believe we have been misled for centuries.

Day 2: Temptation in the Wilderness

Biblical text: Luke 4:1-13 TLV. Key verses: 5-8 "And leading Him up, the devil showed Him all the kingdoms of the world in an instant. And the devil said to Him, *"I'll give to You all this authority along with its glory,* because it has been handed over to me and I can give it to anyone I wish. Therefore, *if you will worship before me, all this shall be Yours."* But answering, Yeshua told him, *"It is written, You shall worship Adonai your God, and Him only shall you serve."*

Who is doing battle with Jesus? The devil offers Jesus "authority along with its glory". Who really has the authority in this battle?

In his attempts to deceive Jesus he offers Jesus authority in exchange for what? In exchange for His worship.

What is Jesus' reply? "You shall worship Adonai your God, and Him only shall you serve." There are only two masters. Whom will you serve?

If satan tested Jesus, why do we think we can avoid being tested too? It matters not our spiritual maturity. We will be tested at every phase of life. Do you understand what it means to "abide" in Christ? (see John 15)

Do you understand the importance of putting on the armor of God? (Ephesians 6:10-18)

Please write out a personal application.

Prayerfully consider the impact of declaring your act of worship! Who do you worship?

Day 3: Spirit of Anti-Messiah

Biblical text: 1 John 2:18 and 4:3 TLV "even now many anti-messiahs have come" and "this is the spirit of the anti-messiah, which you have heard is coming and now is already in the world."

There was a time recently that I realized that John is telling us that many 'anti-messiahs" have "already come" and are "already in the world." He was talking present as in his lifetime. I was always reading this as in sometime in the future.

John is saying, no, anti-messiah has "already" been in the world for centuries.

We could argue for Old Testament validation of the presence of anti-messiah, influencing demons and other demonic activity. I don't believe I would receive much push back. I think we would even agree that through one, sin entered the world, through One, sin was conquered, through one, Jesus was betrayed.

Could we also determine that through one and the complicity of others, many have been misled to accept a change of words that Jesus never intended?

Was King James as power hungry as it appears? (Please see Addendum and do your own research).

Are you aware that King James was the self-appointed head of the church of England? Are you aware that he authored two books during the time of the translating of the King James Bible? (Yes, a Bible version named after himself).

What implications does this information have on the King James Bible? What implications does this information have on everything that is going on globally today?

Do you believe there has been demonic activity influencing presidents, kings, financial institutions, educational leaders at all levels of learning including public and private institutions, medical institutions, justice (at all judicial branches, legal policy makers, reform of prisons, spanning all races and ethnicities, the poor and the widow) and within the community of faith?

Resources: The Bible Project: Justice
https://bibleproject.com/explore/justice/

Prager University:
https://www.prageru.com/playlist/restricted-by-youtube/
Control the words, Control the culture

Please write out a personal application in response to what you have learned.

Please pray over your personal application. May the Holy Spirit lead you into new discovery.

Day 4: Authority

Biblical Text: Matthew 9:1-8 TLV (key verse: verse 8) *"when the crowd saw it, they were afraid and glorified God, who had given such authority to men."* Matthew 28:18-20 And Yeshua came up to them and spoke to them, saying, *"All authority in heaven and on earth has been given to Me. Go therefore and make disciples of all nations, immersing them in the name of the Father and the Son and the Ruach ha-Kodesh, teaching them to observe all I have commanded you. And remember! I am with you always, even to the end of the age."*

What is this authority that is mentioned? Who is it given too? Is it given to Ekklesia or the "church"?

Consider Matthew 10:1-28 before making or drawing conclusions about defining "authority." Is it possible that the church does not experience the power and authority Jesus is giving in this passage, because the church is operating outside of Jesus' given authority which was not given to a church but to the Ekklesia?

Do we need to repent as a follower of Jesus?

Please be cautious about projecting blame onto our spiritual leaders of the past or present. They taught us what they were taught. If we blame them, it would be like us blaming Adam and Eve or blaming the Jews for nailing Jesus to the cross. We all are responsible for our own choices and decisions.

Just like the Bereans who studied the word daily to see if what the Apostles were teaching them are true, we are responsible to study for ourselves whether what we are being taught is true.

Please let us apply grace and share what we have discovered in love.

Please write out a self-discovered application of the scripture you have just read.

Prayerfully consider declaring your application to one another and unto God.

Day 5: A Form of Godliness

Biblical text: 2 Timothy 3:1-17 TLV (key verse: verse 5) "holding to an outward form of godliness but denying its power. Avoid these people."

This is a passage that hit me squarely about 6 years ago. I talk about my story in a book I collaborated on called, Divinely Designed.

In my chapter I share how the Holy Spirit humbled me that day in full repentance and has since restored and repurposed me. And why shouldn't He? He promised us in the conclusion of 2 Timothy 3 to "restore" us. It is one of the powers of scripture that along with forgiving sins, He is able to accomplish in us.

What other powers does Paul tell Timothy (and us) about the Bible? This is part of the transformation that Paul speaks of in Romans 12:2. It is this transformation that leads into the process of "dying to self."

Let us also look inward and allow the Holy Spirit to reveal to us our blind spots and help us to take the log out of our eye first (Matthew 7:5 TLV), "then you will see clearly to take the speck out of your brother's eye."

Likewise, how many of us take seriously Matthew 5: 23-24? Do we reconcile accounts as they occur? Or do we allow them to build up and keep us from relationship?

What does repentance, forgiveness, and dying to self, have to do with the issue of slavery?

Please write out a personal application for each scripture we reviewed.

Prayerfully consider the impact of living an obedient lifestyle.

Day 6: The Consequence of

Biblical text: Revelation 22:18-19 NASB "*I testify to everyone who hears the words of the prophecy of this book. If anyone adds to them, God shall add to him the plagues that are written in this book; and if anyone takes away from the words of the book of this prophecy, God shall take away his share in the Tree of Life and the Holy City, which are written in this book*"

Wow! In the context of the claims that I am making regarding King James and those complicit in translating the King James Bible, we need to consider the words of the Holy Spirit as given to John in the last chapter of Revelation!

Is this the way that the Ekklesia needs to look at the warning given to man regarding the sacredness of the Bible?

Did King James and the scholars that engaged in this gargantuan effort realize what they were conspiring to do? Did the leading theologians of the day from Oxford, Cambridge and Westminster realize what they were complicit in doing?

Notice also that according to the addendum of the document from Wikipedia, "all men were members of the Church of England." Not one of them appears to have spoken up in concern of the changes in words used in place of Ekklesia.

Was this a conspiracy of the highest order within the community of faith?

At the very least it seems obvious that the State was working with the Community of Faith's best Seminarians of the day, but controlling the narrative. This is the concern that I have for today. The world is controlling the narrative, while the Community of Faith appears for the most part to be sitting back.

In what ways has the world hijacked certain icons or words of the Faith Community, and dictated the narrative around education, justice, finances, health, and marriage?

Why is it important to know our True identity?

How can we begin to reclaim what is God's?

Please write out a self-application of what you purpose to do, knowing this information?

Prayerfully consider your next steps.

Day 7: Becoming a Self-Identified Bond Slave of Jesus

Biblical Text: Romans 6:17-23 Key verse: verse 17) *"But thanks be to God that though you were slaves of sin, you were set free from sin, you became enslaved to righteousness. I speak in human terms because of the weakness of your flesh. For just as you yielded your body parts as slaves to uncleanness and lawlessness, leading to more lawlessness, so now yield your body parts as slaves to righteousness, resulting in holiness. For when you were slaves of sin, you were free with regard to righteousness. So then, what outcome did you have that you are now ashamed of? For the end of those things is death. But now, having been set free from sin and having become enslaved to God, you have your fruit resulting in holiness. And the outcome is eternal life. For sin's payment is death, but God's gracious gift is eternal life in Messiah Yeshua our Lord."*

Paul's message is abundantly clear. If you are born again, your ownership as a slave has transferred from one master to your new Master, Jesus. You are owned and bought with His blood! You are no longer bound to your old master and the desires of the flesh. Did you see the word "yield"? It is the same concept that Paul urges all followers of Jesus, to "present" your body as a living offering or "a living sacrifice." He describes it as our "spiritual service."

When was the last time you went to the altar and yielded yourself, laying on the altar and saying, "I am Yours, Lord"?

I provided a list of people in the Bible who self-identified as Bond-slaves of Jesus.

Do you realize that Mary, Jesus' mother proclaimed to the angel of God, "Behold the bond-slave of the Lord, be it done to me according to your word." (Luke 1:38 NASB)

Here is a teenage girl who is being tasked with becoming the mother of Messiah Yeshua. She was not asked if she wanted to be the mother of Yeshua. She was told by the angel of the Lord what was happening to her and she seemingly understood. We are not told that she began crying and saying woe is me. She knew who she was!

All the other self-identified bond-slaves of Jesus knew who they were too. It is critical that we know who we are in Jesus.

It is wonderful to know that we are a "friend of God". But, we are so much more!

I hope that you come to the point in your journey with Jesus, that you too self-identify as a bond-slave of Jesus Christ.

I challenge you to make a list of who you are in Jesus. I will give you the first couple:

I am the righteousness of Jesus (Romans 6:18).

I am a child of God (Romans 8:16).

If you are ready, please write a personal declaration of your identity in Jesus.

Please pray for the decisions of many to become bond-slaves of Jesus!

If you have made a personal declaration of being a bond-slave of Jesus, would you please do me the favor of going to www.Firstplaceministries.com and let us know of your commitment? Thank you.

KING JAMES VERSION (ADDENDUM)

*This Addendum is entirely taken from the section
"Considerations for a new version" on this Wikipedia webpage:
<u>https://en.wikipedia.org/wiki/King_James_Version</u>*

The newly crowned King James convened the Hampton Court Conference in 1604. That gathering proposed a new English version in response to the perceived problems of earlier translations as detected by the Puritan faction of the Church of England. Here are three examples of problems the Puritans perceived with the Bishops and Great Bibles:

> *"First, Galatians iv. 25 (from the Bishops' Bible). The Greek word susoichei is not well translated as now it is, bordereth neither expressing the force of the word, nor the apostle's sense, nor the situation of the place. Secondly, psalm cv. 28 (from the Great Bible), 'They were not obedient;' the original being, 'They were not disobedient.' Thirdly, psalm cvi. 30 (also from the Great Bible), 'Then stood up Phinees and prayed,' the Hebrew hath, 'executed judgment.'"*

Instructions were given to the translators that were intended to limit the Puritan influence on this new translation. The Bishop of London added a qualification that the translators would add no marginal notes (which had been an issue in the Geneva Bible).

King James cited two passages in the Geneva translation where he found the marginal notes offensive to the principles of divinely ordained royal supremacy: Exodus 1:19, where the Geneva Bible notes had commended the example of civil disobedience to the Egyptian Pharaoh showed by the Hebrew midwives, and also II Chronicles 15:16, where the Geneva Bible had criticized King Asa for not having executed his idolatrous 'mother', Queen Maachah (Maachah had actually been Asa's grandmother, but James considered the Geneva Bible reference as sanctioning the execution of his own mother Mary, Queen of Scots).

Further, the King gave the translators instructions designed to guarantee that the new version would conform to the ecclesiology of the Church of England. Certain Greek and Hebrew words were to be translated in a manner that reflected the traditional usage of the church. For example, old ecclesiastical words such as the word "church" were to be retained and not to be translated as "congregation". The new translation would reflect the episcopal structure of the Church of England and traditional beliefs about ordained clergy.

KING JAMES VERSION (ADDENDUM) 69

James' instructions included several requirements that kept the new translation familiar to its listeners and readers. The text of the Bishops' Bible would serve as the primary guide for the translators, and the familiar proper names of the biblical characters would all be retained. If the Bishops' Bible was deemed problematic in any situation, the translators were permitted to consult other translations from a ***pre-approved list***: the Tyndale Bible, the Coverdale Bible, Matthew's Bible, the Great Bible, and the Geneva Bible.

In addition, later scholars have detected an influence on the Authorized Version from the translations of Taverner's Bible and the New Testament of the Douay–Rheims Bible. It is for this reason that the flyleaf of most printings of the Authorized Version observes that the text had been "*translated out of the original tongues, and with the former translations diligently compared and revised, by His Majesty's special commandment.*"

As the work proceeded, more detailed rules were adopted as to how variant and uncertain readings in the Hebrew and Greek source texts should be indicated, including the requirement that words supplied in English to 'complete the meaning' of the originals should be printed in a different type face.

The task of translation was undertaken by 47 scholars, although 54 were originally approved. All were members of the Church of England and all except Sir Henry Savile were clergy. The scholars worked in six committees, two based in each of the University of Oxford, the University of

Cambridge, and Westminster. The committees included scholars with Puritan sympathies, as well as High Churchmen. Forty unbound copies of the 1602 edition of the Bishops' Bible were specially printed so that the agreed changes of each committee could be recorded in the margins.

The committees worked on certain parts separately and the drafts produced by each committee were then compared and revised for harmony with each other. The scholars were not paid directly for their translation work, instead a circular letter was sent to bishops encouraging them to consider the translators for appointment to well-paid livings as these fell vacant. Several were supported by the various colleges at Oxford and Cambridge, while others were promoted to bishoprics, deaneries and prebends through royal patronage.

The committees started work towards the end of 1604. King James VI and I, on 22 July 1604, sent a letter to Archbishop Bancroft asking him to contact all English churchmen requesting that they make donations to his project:

> *"Right trusty and well beloved, we greet you well. Whereas we have appointed certain learned men, to the number of 4 and 50, for the translating of the Bible, and in this number, divers of them have either no ecclesiastical preferment at all, or else so very small, as the same is far unmeet for men of their deserts and yet we in ourself in any convenient time cannot well remedy*

it, therefor we do hereby require you, that presently you write in our name as well to the Archbishop of York, as to the rest of the bishops of the province of Cant.[erbury] signifying unto them, that we do well and straitly charge every one of them ... that (all excuses set apart) when a prebend or parsonage ... shall next upon any occasion happen to be void ... we may commend for the same some such of the learned men, as we shall think fit to be preferred unto it ... Given unto our signet at our palace of West.[minister] on 2 and 20 July, in the 2nd year of our reign of England, France, and of Ireland, and of Scotland xxxvii."

They had all completed their sections by 1608, the Apocrypha committee finishing first. From January 1609, a General Committee of Review met at Stationers' Hall, London to review the completed marked texts from each of the six committees. The General Committee included John Bois, Andrew Downes and John Harmar, and others known only by their initials, including "AL" (who may be Arthur Lake), and were paid for their attendance by the Stationers' Company. John Bois prepared a note of their deliberations (in Latin) – which has partly survived in two later transcripts. Also surviving of the translators' working papers are a bound-together set of marked-up corrections to one of the forty Bishops' Bibles—covering the Old Testament and Gospels, and also a manuscript translation of the text of the Epistles, excepting those verses where no change was being recommended to the readings in the

Bishops' Bible. Archbishop Bancroft insisted on having a final say making fourteen further changes, of which one was the term "bishopricke" at Acts 1:20.

15 RULES OF TRANSLATION FOR THE KING JAMES VERSION (KJV)

This following segment is entirely taken from this webpage:
https://www.petergoeman.com/15-rules-of-translation-for-the-king-james-version-kjv/

When King James commissioned the King James Version, he approved 15 principles of translation which were instituted by Richard Bancroft, the bishop of London in 1604. These translation principles are as follows:

1. The ordinary Bible read in the Church, commonly called the Bishops Bible, to be followed, and as little altered as the Truth of the original will permit.

2. The names of the Prophets, and the Holy Writers, with the other Names of the Text, to be retained, as nigh as may be, accordingly as they were vulgarly used.

3. The Old Ecclesiastical Words to be kept, viz. the Word Church not to be translated Congregation &c.

4. When a Word hath divers Significations, that to be kept which hath been most commonly used by the most of the Ancient Fathers, being agreeable to the Propriety of the Place, and the Analogy of the Faith.

5. The Division of the Chapters to be altered, either not at all, or as little as may be, if Necessity so require.

6. No Marginal Notes at all to be affixed, but only for the explanation of the Hebrew or Greek Words, which cannot without some circumlocution, so briefly and fitly be expressed in the Text.

7. Such Quotations of Places to be marginally set down as shall serve for the fit Reference of one Scripture to another.

8. Every particular Man of each Company, to take the same Chapter or Chapters, and having translated or amended them severally by himself, where he thinketh good, all to meet together, confer what they have done, and agree for their Parts what shall stand.

9. As any one Company hath dispatched any one Book in this Manner they shall send it to the rest, to be considered of seriously and judiciously, for His Majesty is very careful in this Point.

10. If any Company, upon the Review of the Book so sent, doubt or differ upon any Place, to send them

15 RULES OF TRANSLATION FOR THE KING JAMES VERSION (KJV)

Word thereof; note the Place, and withal send the Reasons, to which if they consent not, the Difference to be compounded at the general Meeting, which is to be of the chief Persons of each Company, at the end of the Work.

11. When any Place of special Obscurity is doubted of Letters to be directed by Authority, to send to any Learned Man in the Land, for his Judgement of such a Place.

12. Letters to be sent from every Bishop to the rest of his Clergy, admonishing them of this Translation in hand; and to move and charge as many skillful in the Tongues; and having taken pains in that kind, to send his particular Observations to the Company, either at Westminster, Cambridge, or Oxford.

13. The Directors in each Company, to be the Deans of Westminster, and Chester for that Place; and the King's Professors in the Hebrew or Greek in either University.

14. These translations to be used when they agree better with the Text than the Bishops Bible: Tyndale's, Matthew's, Coverdale's, Whitchurch's, Geneva.

15. Besides the said Directors before mentioned, three or four of the most Ancient and Grave Divines, in either of the Universities, not employed in

> Translating, to be assigned by the vice-Chancellor, upon Conference with the rest of the Heads, to be Overseers of the Translations as well Hebrew as Greek, for the better observation of the 4th Rule above specified.

Translation rules 1, 6, and 14 are interesting. Rule #1 mandated that their translation uses the Bishop's Bible as a base text whenever possible. This was likely because the Bishop's translation was the official Bible of the Church. However, Tyndale's translation ended up being far more influential, accounting for 4/5 (80%) of the KJV New Testament.

Rule #6 mandated no study notes in the margins of the new translation. The Geneva Bible (which was the most popular English translation of the time) had many marginal notations, some of which King James read as challenges to his royal authority. This was the main motivation for a new translation. Thus, the KJV translation was limited from study notes.

Translation rule #14 gives further evidence for the fact that the intention was for the KJV translation to be more of a revision of existing English translations than a new translation. The translators utilized the existing English texts where possible.

Against those who claim the KJV translation is inspired, I have written about how the KJV is not without error. Here we also note that the KJV itself was not a revolutionary translation. Rather, it was largely a compilation of already-existing translations.

ROLLAND WRIGHT

Rolland is the Founder and President of First Place Ministries. He holds a Bachelor's degree in Christian Education from Biola University.

He is also the Founder and President of The Widows Project and the published author of the book The Widows Project: Serving the Widowed with the Father's Heart.

Rolland enjoys writing and playing various board or card games. Social engagements are always on the calendar with friends.

His two (2) life verses are Acts 17:28 (TLV) "for in Him we live and move and have our being" and Colossians 1:18b (NASB) "that He might come to have first place in everything."

Rolland has a son Chris married to Cindy (2 daughters Chloe & Brenna); 2 daughters, Jennifer married to Nick (son Carter & daughter Kaylee) and Bethany (daughter Brooke). Rolland's parents, celebrated their 68th wedding anniversary in June 2020.

Photo Credit: Kai Chinn
BHGM Photography

PLEASE RATE MY BOOK

I would be honored if you would take a few moments to rate our book on Amazon.com.

A five-star rating and a short comment ("Very informative!" or "I know at least 3 people who could benefit from this book!") would be much appreciated. I welcome longer, positive comments as well.

If you feel like this book should be rated at three stars or fewer, please hold off posting your comments on Amazon.

Instead, please send your feedback directly to me, so that I could use it to improve the next edition. I'm committed to providing the best value to our readers, and your thoughts can make that possible.

You can reach me at Rolland@firstplceministries.com.

Thank you very much,

Rolland Wright
President & Founder, First Place Ministries
www.firstplaceministries.com